So You Want to Be a Patient Advocate?

Choosing a Career in Health or Patient Advocacy
Third Edition

by
Trisha Torrey,
Every Patient's Advocate

So You Want to Be a Patient Advocate?
Choosing a Career in Health or Patient Advocacy
Third Edition

ISBN: 978-0-9828014-5-1

DiagKNOWsisMedia.com

Trisha Torrey, Every Patient's Advocate
352-459-0509
contact@diagKNOWsis.com

Discounts for bulk-orders of this book are available by contacting the author. Trisha Torrey is also available for speaking opportunities to groups of patients or professionals.

DiagKNOWsis Media
Leesburg, Florida
www.DiagKNOWsisMedia.com

Also from DiagKNOWsis Media:

♦ You Bet Your Life! The 10 Mistakes Every Patient Makes
  (How to Fix Them to Get the Healthcare You Deserve)

♦ You Bet Your Life! The Top 10 Reasons You Need a Professional Patient
  Advocate by Your Side

This book is #1 in the series for Health and Patient Advocates.
Also available:

2. The Health Advocate's Start and Grow Your Own Practice Handbook

3. The Health Advocate's Basic Marketing Handbook

4. The Health Advocate's Advanced Marketing Handbook

Printed in the United States of America

Table of Contents

> **Bonus!**
>
> $5 off the next book in this series:
> *The Health Advocate's Start and Grow Your Own Practice Handbook*
> **See page 47.**

Chapter One

The World Needs Patient Advocates

C hanneling Forest Gump here: health care is like a box of chocolates. We never know what we're going to get.

Patients enter the healthcare system with difficult symptoms or to prevent health problems from cropping up later.

Sometimes they get exactly what they need with no hiccups whatsoever.

But too often:

- Problems crop up – some of which can be solved in the short term, and some which require far more effort to overcome.

- They get what they need in the short term, but wish for additional support to weather future storms.

- Solutions are offered by providers but payers stand in the way.

- Their safety and well-being are jeopardized, leading to medical mistakes which cause injury, extended illness, or even create new medical problems..

- They unnecessarily die or go into bankruptcy.

Not unlike that box of chocolates, we never know what our outcomes are going to be, not all of them are to our liking (does anyone else think the chocolate covered cherry tastes like cough syrup?), and some are unpalatable all together.

Further, even for those who think they've gotten what they need, sans hiccups, they may be fooled without realizing it. Undisclosed errors, medical bills which arrive months, or even a year later. (You know – like when you grab that yummy vanilla crème only to find out it's full of nuts?)

Guide Dogs and Watch Dogs

I won't go into the details or all the reasons the healthcare system has become so dysfunctional, or the many ways it creates hurdles big and small for patients. Those problems are outlined in other books.[1]

Instead, this book is an overview of the people who offer solutions; professional patient advocates. The more hurdles put in the way of patients, the more confusing the system, the more onerous or dangerous it becomes, the more we need advocacy professionals to help them navigate the system successfully.

Enter health and patient advocates and navigators, who, like guide dogs and watch dogs, protect patients and keep them safe. They prevent problems or fix problems, hold providers' toes to the fire, coordinate care, and make sure that care patients do receive doesn't create a financial tailspin for them.

Please note the contrast with healthcare personnel that work within the system, mostly in clinical positions. In fairness, the great majority of providers, including doctors, nurses, advanced practice nurses, physician assistants, the many nursing roles and others – they are all advocates of a sort. They are direct medical advocates.

But they have some real constraints imposed on them through that same system – services they can't or won't provide because of the money implications (see Chapter Four: The Allegiance Factor.)

The professional advocate role is intended to balance those constraints. When problems crop up, advocates are there to fix them. And if problems are likely to crop up, advocates can be there to prevent them.

Important! Note that an advocacy role is *not* a medical role.

For example, if you want to drive to Denver, you need someone who knows the route, someone who can and will pack your suitcase, someone else to drive the car, and someone who is willing, and can afford to do so, to pay for the gas. Those are all very different aspects of a road trip to Denver. They may or may not be performed by the same person.

Professional advocates fulfill the role of knowing the route from beginning to end, and safely navigating patients along it. They won't necessarily pack the suitcase or fill the gas tank. Doctors may prescribe the route, but they certainly don't drive the patient there; nor do any other providers fulfill that role.

Needed: More Advocates to Fill the Gaps—Maybe YOU!

In recent years, there has been more recognition of the problems the healthcare system creates for patients. The media regularly reports on obstacles and insults delivered to patients. We talk to friends and family and learn about their difficult experiences. Or we

---

1   *You Bet Your Life! The 10 Mistakes Every Patient Makes (How to Fix Them to Get the Healthcare You Deserve)* http://bit.ly/YouBet

suffer at the hands of the system ourselves, and experience firsthand how extremely difficult it is (if not impossible) for patients to get what they need.

Of course, healthcare is big business. The goals of all providers, facilities and suppliers, are to either suck as much money as possible out of the patients who need their products and services, or to save as much money as it can in the delivery of those products and services. Even outside the United States, in countries where the government pays for all care, the goals remain the same. They may not be trying to profit in the same ways, but their budgets must always be stretched.

Those profitability and efficiency goals are at the very core of most problems imposed on patients.[2] They want either the most expensive route to Denver (so they can make more money) or the cheapest route to Denver (so they can save more money) – but no one is guiding the patient to choose the right route for her, on her terms. That's where professional advocates come in.

Lately we have seen the introduction of new technology solutions that are intended to keep patients safer, and sometimes to make the actual delivery of care more efficient. Some are effective, such as systems set up to prevent the prescribing of the wrong drug, or a wrong or dangerous dose of a drug. Another example of a positive use of technology: Patients can be "seen" through telemedicine for convenience, or to gain access to specialists in far away places.

Unfortunately, though, there is no technology solution for some of the major problems patients experience.

- A hospital patient, confined to a bed after surgery, is hours past when he was supposed to receive his next pain meds, and can't get anyone to answer him even after pushing his call button over and over again.

- A lifesaving but expensive drug, approved by the FDA, is prescribed by the doctor, but not covered by a patient's health insurance, making it unaffordable.

- A patient about to begin chemo hasn't been able to find a doctor for a second opinion.

- Another patient, upon discharge from the hospital, has no one to help her into her home, bring in groceries, or make sure her prescriptions have been filled.

- Still another one has just received a medical bill for thousands of dollars – after only two treatments – and can't understand how that bill can possibly be right.

Of course, I could fill this entire book with similar examples.

Who is supposed to help these folks get what they want and need from the system?

---

2   Those goals notwithstanding, yes, I recognize that no provider, facility or supplier specifically intends to harm patients – their customers. But too many prove by the way they behave and operate that they are willing to sacrifice some patients to achieve what they consider to be their more important goals: profitability, efficiency, and bigger paychecks.

These problems require PEOPLE SOLUTIONS.

Enter Health and patient advocates, navigators, and care managers.

Choosing Advocacy as a Career

There are thousands of patients who navigate the system every day, and not nearly enough advocates available to prevent problems or fix them afterward.

Are you considering becoming one of those people who can be there to help these patients? I hope so. I expect that's why you have purchased this book.

I want to support your choice, but – this is important – you need a realistic view of what the career entails and whether or not you can be successful (by your own definition of successful.)

To help you decide if patient advocacy is the right career for you, I have outlined the basics in this book. It is not an exhaustive discussion of the profession, but it is certainly enough to help you decide whether it's a direction you'd like to take and then, if it is, how to make the best choices for your career path.

In this book you'll find:

- The basic tenets of health and patient advocacy.

- The best personality and ethical traits needed to be a good advocate.

- The different types of advocates, including job availability, pros, cons and resources.

Bottom line: this book contains information you will need to determine if patient advocacy is the best career choice for you.

One more point to make here – a confession, of sorts....

As you will be able to tell from reading this book – I love patient advocates! Their devotion and passion for their work, helping people who so desperately need that help, is often so strong that it's physically visible – seen in the time and effort they put into their work. They are so dedicated to helping the patients who need help that many would prefer to do it for free – their compensation is about the satisfaction of a job well done.

I make this statement regardless of the patient advocate's situation: employed, volunteer, self-employed, other-employed – whatevah.

But I do have a bias, and that will be apparent here, too. While I will give you the straight dope on the profession of advocacy, as objectively as possible, you will see me lean at times toward the independent, private advocate – the advocate who works for his or her patient-client directly with no hospital or insurer or anyone else getting in the way of that relationship.

My bias comes from almost twenty years of observation and understanding, and the founding, in 2009, of the Alliance of Professional Health Advocates – an organization that supports private advocacy. See? I just can't help it.

But none of my bias is a reflection on how much I appreciate every advocate – all advocates who work on behalf of patients no matter in what capacity, no matter how they are compensated, if they are compensated at all. They all play an important role, and I have love in my heart for them all.

So let's get started. There's no time to dally. Patients need you!

Chapter Two

A Patient Advocacy Career at a Glance

What Patient Advocates Do

As long as patients have had problems with their health and needed help with their care, there have been patient or health advocates. From family members or loved ones, to large non-profit organizations, to advocates in hospitals or insurance companies to individual, private advocates – or anyone in between – when someone is sick and needs help, there has often been someone who will step up to help. That's what a patient advocate does.

But in the past decade or two, health care and its payment systems have evolved, or devolved, into a system that is now unrecognizable by most patients or their homegrown advocates. Marcus Welby no longer exists, and trying to get the right care by the old rules just doesn't work.

Here are some comparisons that might sound familiar:

You get arrested for something you didn't do and are thrown into jail. You don't know anything about the penal system, and have no idea what you need to do get out. You don't even know the right questions to ask.	So what do you do?	You call a lawyer.
You receive notice that the IRS (or CRA in Canada) is auditing your tax return. As far as you know you only deducted what was allowed, but you're not the expert.	So what do you do?	You call an accountant.
You decide it's time to buy your first house. You look around and find one you just love! But, now what? How do you get a mortgage? How can you be sure there are no termites? Who is in charge of paying your taxes? What if the plumbing leaks or the heater blows up?	So what do you do?	You call a real estate agent.

In these all-important aspects of life, there is a professional who can step in to fill the needs of someone who feels as if his physical, mental or financial health is in jeopardy. And now, for healthcare challenges, that includes patient advocates.

You are diagnosed with something dire, or your medical bills are far too high and may have errors, or you're afraid to spend the night in the hospital because you've heard about medical errors, or you need advice because you've got a chronic disease to manage, or your pain is out of control and doctors won't help you any more, or, or, or, etc.	So what do you do? You call a patient advocate who will help you get what you need from the system.

Patient Advocates – Titles and Descriptions

Patient advocates go by a variety of names. In some cases what they choose to call themselves depends on a job title, or the work they do. In other cases they choose what they will be called based on personal preference. Here are some of the monikers you might see, all of whom are advocates:

- Patient advocate (or health advocate)
- Patient navigator (or health navigator)
- Consumer health advocate
- Care or case manager or coordinator
- Care or case partner
- Care or case advocate
- Ombudsman
- Eldercare professional
- Family mediator
- Health coach
- Health insurance advisors or disability advisor
- Medical bill reviewer or claims reviewer
- And many more.

For purposes of this book, we will use the title "patient advocate" to represent all these titles and others that may be found in use by the general public.

Services Provided by Patient Advocates

In general, there are categories of services provided by advocates. They range from medical/navigation type advocacy such as that performed by cancer nurse navigators, to hospital bedside advocacy, to handling details like tracking down the right hospital personnel to help an inpatient, to ombudsman-type services that include holding insurance company toes to the claims fire, or accepting complaints about providers.

For an employed advocate, one who receives a paycheck from a healthcare profit center,the services are about customer service, assisting the organization's customers, resolving complaints, and defending and enhancing the reputation of the organization she works for. Learn more about those services in Chapter Five: Getting a Job as a Patient Advocate (Section: What Job Responsibilities Do Employed Patient Advocates Have?)

The list of advocacy services provided by private advocates is long. Certainly not all advocates provide all these services, but this will give you an idea of some of the tasks you might perform if you choose to be an advocate. [3]

- Background Research: Diagnosis, Treatment Options and more
- Dental Advocacy (from dental decisions to billing problems)
- Geriatric / Eldercare or Home Health Services
- Guardianship / Conservatorship / Fiduciary Care
- Hospital Bedside, or Travel / Accompaniment to Appointments
- Integrative, Holistic, Complementary and Alternative Therapies
- Legal Assistance including SSDI (Medical / Healthcare Related)
- Mediation (Helping families manage health-related disagreements)
- Medical / Navigational Assistance (Helping you work with your medical providers.)
- Medical Bill Reviewing and Negotiation / Health Insurance / Payer Assistance
- Mental Health and Substance Abuse Assistance
- Pain Management
- Pregnancy, Birth and Pediatric Assistance
- Prevention (Prescription Drug Review, Health/Wellness Coaching, Weight Loss, Immunity, Others)
- Shared Decision Making
- Health Insurance Consulting

Patient Advocacy Certification: An Important Step Forward

One question asked frequently by those considering advocacy as a career regards certification. They want to know how to become certified, or whether they need a license to practice advocacy, or whether a specific course they have found online offers certification, or whether that certification is 'real' – and more.

Why is that important to them? Because they recognize that being certified means they will be held to a standard of professionalism. That standard is important for not just the status of advocacy, but it also helps patients understand there is a standard of ethics and practice they can expect when tapping into the services of an advocate.

---

3 https://advoconnection.com/advocacy-services/

In 2018 certification became available for advocates.

Developed by the Patient Advocate Certification Board, the new credential demands deep knowledge of the profession's ethical principles, it's standards, best practices, the law, health care system basics, and more. Those who pass the PACB's rigorous exam earn their BCPA designation, Board Certified Patient Advocate.

You can stay up-to-date on advocacy certification, and register to take the next exam, at the PACB's website: www.PACBoard.org

Licensure is something else all together. Licenses are generally issued by governments (state or local) and only give permission for someone to practice their craft, and are often unrelated to whether that person has the skills required.

As of 2022, no state or local governments license advocates.

The Patient Advocacy General Employment Landscape

If you decided to be a lawyer, or a real estate agent, or an accountant, or any other personal service provider, you would have a small handful of general choices of employment in that profession. The same is true for this very personal profession of patient advocacy.

Employers

If you are looking for a regular paycheck, or generally prefer not to be self-employed, then finding an employer who will hire you as an advocate is your goal.

Find more information about patient advocate employment in Chapter Five: Getting a Job as a Patient Advocate.

Self-Employment

Being self-employed, developing one's own advocacy practice, is a great approach to combining advocacy work with the independence of choosing which patients you might want to work with.

Learn more about starting and growing a private advocacy practice in Chapter Six: Patient Advocates in Private Practice.

Chapter Three

Do You Have the Personality and Skills to Be a Good Patient Advocate?

I promise, this overview isn't going to sound like the mean girls in high school assessing whether or not you are cool. By my measure, the fact that you are considering entering into such a worthwhile helping profession by itself makes you one of the cool kids.

But the nature of patient advocacy most definitely requires certain skills and traits, some in more abundance than others. As we go through them[4], you'll see why this is important.

The lists in this chapter are very general, applying to all advocates, regardless of employment prospects. Those which are specific to your choice of employment are included in the appropriate chapters later in this book.

Your Advocacy Personality

» You must be a people person.

Patient advocacy isn't really about medicine or science or insurance or billing. It's about people who have problems with those aspects of their healthcare. Genuinely liking people – even people who may be upset, frustrated, cranky, angry, sick or hurt, or any other

---

4   These traits have been borrowed and edited from *The Health Advocate's Start and Grow Your Own Practice Handbook*, Chapters One and Two.

emotion – and being able to work with them under those circumstances, is paramount. If you don't like to work with people, you won't like being a patient advocate.

Do you get along with people even when they are difficult or at their worst?

» You must be a good listener.

One of the most important people skills you'll need is the ability to listen. When a patient or caregiver comes to you for help, they are not coming to hear YOUR stories, or YOUR experiences. They are hiring you to listen to THEM. Active listening, which sometimes includes the ability to "hear between the lines" is one of the most important skills you need to bring to your advocacy work.

Do you listen to others well? Are you an active listener?

» You must be empathetic, compassionate, and patient.

When patients and caregivers are hurting, or upset, or frustrated, or angry – or even when they are happy and grateful – they are still people who will share all those emotions verbally and physically.

Studies show that most patients feel as if they don't get nearly the amount of compassion or empathy they wish to get (and used to get) from their providers. It's a big reason private advocacy is growing so quickly – it's filling that empathy void.

No matter how you deliver your advocacy services, whether through an employer, or through your own private practice, or even as volunteer, empathy and compassion need to rule every step you take, every conversation you have, the decisions and recommendations you make, and most importantly, the way you deliver those messages. Empathy rules.

Would others identify you as an empathetic, compassionate, and patient person?

» You must be ethical and trustworthy.

People will come to you with their most intimate problems – problems that regard their health and their money. They must be instantly able to trust that you can help them.

Further, you must know what you stand for, being sure you do your work guided clearly by what is right and what is wrong. Too many other healthcare professions have yielded their ethics to money, or to marching to the tune of the money-holders requirements. (Learn more about this in Chapter Four: Standards, Ethics and the Allegiance Factor.)

Do you have an honest face, voice, and demeanor?

Do other people trust you quickly?

» You must be a creative problem solver and decision-maker.

There are two kinds of people in any workplace: those who wait around for someone to tell them what to do, and those who just get the job done, taking initiative, making decisions, trying new approaches, pulling out the stops to solve every sort of problem, and trusting their intuition that they are making good choices.

As a patient or health advocate, your creative problem solving and decision making chops will be tested on a constant basis.

Are you confident and creative enough to face challenges, develop creative solutions, and make good decisions?

» You must be a confident communicator.

When people are sick or frightened or unsure, they want to know that someone who isn't those things is looking out for them – that the caregiving someone, the advocate, has confidence in the information and recommendations begin made. Their advocate's confidence gives them a bit more confidence of their own. That's a real gift in a healthcare world of uncertainty.

Now, I don't mean false confidence. I mean accurate, confidence-inducing communication.

Here are some examples of the differences:

Challenge	Over-confident	Under-confident	Just right
Mrs. Jones is upset because her hospital bill is far higher than she expected.	Sure Mrs. Jones – I can easily cut your hospital bill in half!	Gee I don't know Mrs. Jones. I hate asking those folks in the billing department for help. They give me the evil eye.	Sure Mrs. Jones. I'll work with the billing department to be sure these charges are accurate. If they aren't, we'll work to correct them.
Mr. Brown is upset because his wife has been diagnosed with breast cancer.	Oh Mr. Brown, I'm sure she'll survive this just fine. We'll find a second opinion doctor who will reverse this diagnosis and then you won't have to worry about it any more.	Gee Mr. Brown, I am so sorry to hear about your wife's diagnosis. I'm not sure if there is anything I can do to help you or her. Chemo and radiation are just horrible experiences.	Well Mr. Brown. I can imagine you and your wife are probably quite anxious over all this. Let's confirm her diagnosis with a second opinion doctor, then if it's confirmed, discuss which treatment option is her preference once she has all the facts in front of her.

I hope the ideas of confidence and expectation management are clear to you.

Are you a good, confident communicator?

» You must have a thick skin.

No doubt you've heard the truism that you can't please everyone all the time, and there is no place that is truer than in advocacy. Further, for all the reasons cited in this chapter—when people are sick, and cranky, and their very life and financial stability are being threatened, they are bound to be times that even the simplest of problems seem overwhelming. And when your patient "ain't happy – ain't nobody happy."

You need the ability to understand that in most cases, their dissatisfaction isn't personal – it's how they are coping. Because you represent all the steps and emotions that they must cope with, you may be the target of their discontent more often than you can imagine.

It may take a while to develop those emotional calluses, and even better, develop that balance between being calloused and being empathetic. But a true professional knows how to balance those two successfully for both her own benefit and her patient's.

How thick is your skin?

» You must understand which side of your bread your butter is on – and proceed accordingly.

I know – this one seems a bit cryptic. It will remain so until Chapter Four: Standards, Ethics, and the Allegiance Factor. It's so important, it requires its own chapter.

Your Advocacy Skills and Knowledge

In some ways, skills and knowledge are easier to quantify. They are most certainly easier to develop even if they haven't been a part of who you are to this point in your life.

Advocacy skills are, basically, customer service skills, health and health system knowledge, and people and communication skills.

- Knowledge of how the healthcare system works
- Knowledge of how patients and caregivers think, and the ability to put oneself in their shoes (empathy and point of view)
- Knowledge of doctors' offices, hospitals, other facilities and healthcare organizations function

- Knowledge of how insurance and public payment systems (Medicaid, Medicare) work, both for and against patients

- Health system navigation knowledge

- Knowledge of HIPAA basics

- Shared decision making skills

- Billing, insurance claims and reimbursement systems knowledge

- Creative problem solving

- Research skills and good resources– for learning about diagnoses or treatment options, finding good professionals to work with and more

- Professionalism

- A solid commitment to, and understanding of customer service tenets

- Good telephone manners

- Well-spoken

- Strong handshake (an air of confidence)

- Facilitation / negotiation / bargaining/mediation skills for working with patients and their loved ones, or encouraging medical personal to see things through the eyes of the patient

Notice this list of skills is not medical. I am often asked whether it is necessary to have a clinical background and experience. Doctors, nurses, nurse practitioners, physician assistants, and other clinical roles can provide good medical background knowledge for advocacy, but since advocacy isn't medical, those skills won't be called upon in the ways you might expect.

In other words (loud and clear!) **No! You do not have to be a physician or nurse to be an effective and successful patient advocate!**[5]

In fact, as of 2022, if you listed the top 25 successful independent advocates in the United States, more than half had no clinical background before they chose their advocacy career.

In many cases, the skills or knowledge you need must have been developed in other jobs or experiences you've had before now. Many are skills you can learn by taking classes or working with a mentor.

If you identify an employer you'd like to work with (find more about this in Chapter Five: Getting a Job as a Patient Advocate) there may be additional skills and experience they seek.

---

5   There may be times medical knowledge can help you help a patient-client. If you don't have the medical background needed, you will have developed a resource bank of people who do have that medical knowledge and can be called upon to help your patient.

For Independent Advocates – Business Skills

The skills listed to this point have been about advocacy itself. They are needed no matter what flavor of advocacy you might choose for your career.

Since the early 2000s, the fastest growing delivery systems for patient advocacy has been independent, professional, private advocacy – advocates who are self-employed, work with patients and their caregivers directly, and are paid by them directly.

In order to succeed as an independent advocate, your business skills must be developed and honed just as your advocacy skills are. You will most likely be self-employed, and will need to be able to start and grow a private practice.

Find that additional list of business skills in Chapter Six: Patient Advocates in Private Practice, where they are covered in depth.

Filling the Gaps

If you find you have most of the knowledge and skills from this list, you'll be ready to continue with your decision-making about advocacy as a career.

If you haven't had a chance to learn the skills you'll need, you'll find more than three dozen universities, colleges and organizations that teach advocacy courses.

> **There are links to additional information throughout this book.**
> **To make them easier to access, I've put them all together, online,**
> **so you can just click on them rather than typing them out.**
>
> **Find access information on page 46 of this book.**

Chapter Four

Standards, Ethics, and the Allegiance Factor

I n the Marcus Welby[6] days of healthcare past, we never questioned whether our doctors and nurses had the purest of intentions in diagnosing and treating us. Because most of us had an employer who picked up the tab for all our care, we didn't have to think about the cost of that care. Symptoms meant a trip to the GP, maybe a referral to a specialist, we were taken care of in our own time frame, and then we got on with life.

Fast-forward to today and that scenario has become totally foreign to us. No matter the reason for the need to see a doctor, or be tested or hospitalized, it's no longer just about the goal of getting well. Now it's about the goal of making sure we get what we need, that we have the opportunity to ask the questions that need to be asked, and get the answers that are correct and fair, that choices aren't being made based on the how much money can be made or saved, that we don't suffer from a medical error or infection, and that in the end we don't go bankrupt from it.

During the past 20 years or so we have gone from a healthcare system grounded in paternalism and trust, to a system of second-guessing, double-checking—and fear.

Sadly, the roots of those negatives often stem from conflicts of interest.

Meaning... that **much of the work patient advocates do is about preventing or overcoming those conflicts of interest. Further, that work may potentially create a conflict of interest all its own.**

---

6   Not familiar with Marcus Welby? He was the kindly 1070s TV doctor played by Robert Young. He had all the knowledge and empathy anyone would ever want from a doctor. He took as much time to solve a medical (and sometimes social or family problem) that anyone could ever hope for, and it was always solved within that one-hour program. Learn more about Marcus Welby, MD at https://www.imdb.com/title/tt0063927/

To explore this statement and its effect on the work of advocates, we have to follow the money.

Follow the Money:
Conflicts of Interest Give Rise to Problems in the Healthcare System

In the United States, healthcare is delivered with a profit motive. From health insurers, to providers, hospitals and other facilities, to pharmaceutical and medical device companies, to the online business that sells wheelchairs or even bandages – professional participants in healthcare are just trying to make a buck or save a buck, in pursuit of the almighty bottom line – profitability. Doctors make more money by treating more, or treating with more expensive treatments. Hospitals make money by keeping higher-paying patients there longer. Insurers make more money by denying care and claims. Pharmaceutical and medical device companies charge more – the list goes on. Remember, the entire system is set up to suck as much money as possible from the patients it is set up to serve.

In other countries with more socialized healthcare systems, the story is not so different. It's not a story of profitability to the same extent it is in the US (although for pharmaceutical companies and others it remains so). Instead it's a question of saving money – of not spending money on any more care than is needed. Doctors and other providers are paid salaries, so they don't make more money by prescribing or treating more and more. Hospitals and other facilities have budgets to balance, but they operate under the auspices of the government which provides strict barriers on expenditures. The check and balance there is only that politicians don't get elected when taxes go up. So, whereas in the US, it is payers that put the kibosh on direct healthcare spending, it's the politicians who do so in other countries.

These are all conflicts of interest that may interfere with a patient's care, and that patient advocates must overcome every day as a core focus of their work.

But there is one other conflict of interest that looms even larger to most patient advocates – but not all.

That is, for patient advocates who work for an employer – a hospital, an insurer, a doctor's office – anyone who can limit the lengths an advocate can go to for his/her patient – that limitation becomes its own conflict of interest.

- A hospital advocate is approached by a patient who needs help dealing with an arrogant surgeon. But the arrogant surgeon, who makes millions for that hospital each year, has so much clout that the patient advocate could lose her job or be demoted by crossing him. She knows this is true because she has watched it happen with two others. So how can that advocate serve the patient through the hospital? She probably cannot.

- A caregiver calls the insurance company for her husband. She is transferred by customer service to the insurance company's advocate, a nurse. The patient explains that her husband's doctor wants him to see a sub-specialist because it's believed he has Disease X. The nurse advocate knows immediately that the patient will need to see a sub-specialist and will probably need an expensive course of treatment. But she is not allowed to approve that sort of visit. No doctor who sub-specializes in that problem is included in that insurer's network. The only way the nurse advocate can serve the patient is to tell the caregiver that such a visit will be out-of-network, costing the patient thousands, if not tens of thousands of dollars. So how can the insurance company advocate serve the patient? She probably cannot.

- A nurse navigator working at the cancer center in a large regional hospital is assigned a new breast cancer patient. Her job is to shepherd that patient through her treatment, making sure she gets what she needs, when she needs it. But it becomes very clear to her that the treatment prescribed is not what the patient wishes – it is what the patient was told would be done. The patient is 78 years old and tells the navigator she really doesn't want reconstruction surgery. But when the nurse navigator questions the reconstruction on the patient's behalf she is brushed off and told to "just do her job." So how can the hospital-employed navigator serve the patient? She probably cannot.

All three of these stories have been shared with me by practicing advocates.

All three of these stories showcase the frustrating and potentially dangerous effect defined by the Allegiance Factor.

What Is the Allegiance Factor?

It's a simple concept: If an advocate's paycheck is dependent on an employer who profits from healthcare delivery, then his primary allegiance must be to his employer and not to the patient who needs help.[7]

- A hospital advocate is paid by the hospital which makes money from insurance reimbursements – the emphasis is on bringing in as much money as it can from those reimbursements but not spending any more money than it has to. Thus its advocates can only go so far in their support of helping the patient get what he or she needs.

  By the way – hospital advocates most frequently report to the Risk Management department in the hospital, where all the lawyers work. Their job is to balance the needs of the patient against the potential for a lawsuit.

- An insurance advocate is paid by the insurer which makes money from patient premiums – the emphasis is on keeping those premiums and not incurring any more expense than is necessary. Thus its advocates are limited in the recommendations they make to their customers. (Ask yourself: would you want the people who are trying not to spend one extra dime on your care to be making decisions about how you can, or cannot, be tested or treated?)

---

7   OK – my first real disclaimer here. These are generalizations, and even though the stories come from real life examples, they aren't true of every advocate working for an employer with profit motives (or government that is trying to keep taxation at a minimum.)

- A pharmaceutical company advocate gets paid by the pharmaceutical company which must sell more drugs to patients to make its profits, and does so through enticing doctors to prescribe its drugs. Thus its advocates are looking for ways to support the company's need to increase sales and will cover up problems so that external audiences don't hear about them.

  By the way, these advocates are usually tied to the pharmaceutical or medical device company's marketing department.

- A non-profit organization gets paid by donations, the great majority of which come from pharmaceutical companies (see above.) Thus, the advocate is either encouraged to support treatment, or forbidden to not support it.

Those are just a few examples. The list could go on and on.

On the other hand, if the advocate is working directly for the patient, and being paid directly by the patient or someone else with fiduciary interest in the patient (a parent, an adult child, a trust, a church, even some employers who will benefit from the patient's better health), then the advocate's sole allegiance is to that patient. This is the situation for self-employed, independent patient-direct advocates. This is also the situation for volunteer advocates. It is the relationship which means the conflict-of-interest does not exist.

Thus, the Allegiance Factor underscores the foundational conflict of interest that rules most relationships in healthcare, including that relationship between employed advocates and their patients, but not those advocates who work directly for patients and are paid directly by those patients.

So why have I spent so much time outlining these conflicts of interest? There are a handful of reasons why they belong in this book:

- They are the reason many people who already work in healthcare wish to pursue private advocacy. I hear this from new members of the Alliance of Professional Health Advocates frequently. If allegiance is one reason you are considering private advocacy – then I applaud you.

- Allegiance is one reason not all advocates are created equal. This is actually a subset of reason #1. I can't tell you how many times I have heard from frustrated patients who have tried to work with a hospital or health insurance advocate but were not able to get the help they needed.

- Allegiance is one of the foundations of good advocacy. If you always focus your allegiance on your patient-client, even if you have limits imposed by an employer, you will find far more job satisfaction than you otherwise would.

Allegiance Factor: The Health Advocates' Code of Conduct and Professional Standards

Understanding the potential conflicts in how advocates work with their patients, how can we let our patients know we will do our best not to let those conflicts interfere with our work and devotion, to the patients who trusts us to help them?

Now that advocates have the ability to earn a certification that is based on standards and ethics, the simple answer is: get certified to prove your devotion.

But not all advocates are certified. Further, if you're just getting started, it may be many months before you are eligible to earn certification.

Enter the Code of Conduct and Professional Standards.

The first attempt to outline such guidance came about in 2010 by H. Kenneth Schueler[8] who put together the first code of standards for advocates through an early advocacy organization called NAHAC (pronounced "nack"), the National Association of Health Advocacy Consultants.[9] Ken's proposed standards were then discussed by NAHAC in late 2010, but were not adopted right then, in favor of further study. Eventually NAHAC did adopt a code of ethics.

A year later, as the roots of private advocacy spread deeper, a group of advocates came together through the Alliance of Professional Health Advocates to weave Schueler's standards into the fabric of advocacy, for all advocates, not just those who were members of NAHAC. The Health Advocates' Code of Conduct and Professional Standards was published online and anyone who calls him or herself an advocate is invited to subscribe. The standards address many aspects of advocacy and are important for anyone interested in a career in advocacy to review.

You too are invited to subscribe: www.aphadvocates.org/health-advocate-code/ There is no cost to do so; just a belief in the standards and a desire to make that belief public.

Then, in 2018, the Patient Advocate Certification Board (PACB) launched with its own Code of Ethics, taking the existing codes into account, and making them a standard for certification. Find their code here: www.pacboard.org/code-of-ethics/

You've probably heard it said: if you don't stand for something, you'll fall for anything.[10] A profession like patient or health advocacy where conflicts of interest so directly affect health, life, and life savings, requires a code, a list of important beliefs, in order to bring some standardization to the expectations of the profession.

---

8 Learn more about Ken Schueler: www.SchuelerAward.com

9 NAHAC is an organization that focuses on direct advocacy work. www.NAHAC.com

10 Quote attributed to three people: Alexander Hamilton, Peter Marshall and Malcolm X.

There are links to additional information throughout this book.
To make them easier to access, I've put them all together, online,
so you can just click on them rather than typing them out.

Find access information on page 46 of this book.

Chapter Five

Getting a Job as a Patient Advocate

Among the two or three top questions I am asked through the Alliance of Professional Health Advocates is: where can I get a job as a patient advocate? – or variations thereof, like, if I want to be a patient advocate, what are my job prospects?

Those questions are quickly followed by, "how much money can I make as a patient advocate?"

Of course, the answers to all of them are, "it depends."

So that's what this chapter is for. Let's look at those dependencies.

Who Are the Employers?

It depends. Let's begin with a list:

- Hospitals
- Insurance companies
- Large physician practices
- Outpatient clinics, day surgery centers, or other facilities that serve patients directly
- Skilled nursing, assisted living, senior care and rehab centers
- Home health agencies
- Pharmaceutical and medical device companies that use advocates to liaison with patients
- Law practices which deal with clients' medical needs, like eldercare, disability, medical malpractice, workers comp, personal injury and others.
- Government entities like county or state health departments or social services

- Non-profit organizations
- Large churches and synagogues
- Patient advocacy companies[11]
- Others with similar missions – supplying healthcare services with an interest in the customer service aspects of those services.

Of course, who the employers are depends on what employers are established in the place you want to live, and what your qualifications are for doing the jobs they offer.

Depending on the kind of advocacy work you want to do, you'll find these jobs available throughout the United States.

There are far fewer patient advocacy jobs in Canada, at least using the titles listed in this book. In fact there are so few positions available based on advocacy, I recommend you jump straight to Chapter Six: Patient Advocates in Private Practice.

What Job Responsibilities Do Employed Patient Advocates Have?

Depending on the employer's goals, there are a variety of job duties performed by patient advocates including:

- Protecting the organization and its policies. Most employed advocates work for the risk management (legal) department of the organization, and their focus is on keeping that organization out of hot water. This is not true for navigators— see Notes on the term "navigator" at the end of this chapter.
- Attempting to resolve and document patient and caregiver complaints
- Helping patients and families understand their rights
- Improving patient and family impressions of the organization's quality and reputation
- Keeping the legal department informed of unresolved complaints

How Much Money Can You Make as a Patient Advocate?

Of course, finding a job that pays what you wish to make, or can afford to accept, is a bigger challenge.

Again, the answer to how much you can make depends. It depends on how much experience you have, how much education and training you have, and where you are located.

So here I will generalize, with a few examples from which you can extrapolate:[12]

---

11 These are companies that are in the business of providing advocates to patients. They are not reimbursement based; rather, someone like an employer or union is paying them to help patients as their only business.

TITLE	EDUCATION/EXPERIENCE	ANNUAL SALARY [12] (full time)
Patient Registrar, hospital	High school, no experience needed	Median: $43,000 (entry level)
Patient Appointment Scheduler, large provider practice	High school plus 2 to 5 years experience	Median: $40,000 (entry level)
Patient Representative, insurance	Bachelors plus 2 to 5 years experience	Range: $35,000 to $74,000
Case Manager or Care Manager, hospital, home health or insurance	Bachelors and possibly RN, plus 2 to 5 years experience	Range: $73,000 to $105,000
Patient Navigator, hospital*	BSN, Masters preferred plus 3 to 5 years oncology experience	Range: $41,000 to $60,000
Patient Relations Representative	High school plus 15+ years experience	Median: $65,000
Manager, Patient Advocacy, pharmaceutical industry	Bachelors plus at least 5 years experience including 3 years managerial experience	Median: $95,000
Patient Relations Director, hospital	Bachelor's Degree plus 5 to 10 years experience	Median: $125,000
Director of Advocacy, non-profit	Bachelors, masters preferred, plus minimum 5 years experience in federal legislation and advocacy	Range: $95,000 to $166,000

* See Patient Navigator description in the Miscellany (last) section of this chapter

What Skills or Education Do You Need to be Hired?

You already know the answer to this question. It depends.

Begin with the list of skills found in Chapter Three: Do You Have the Personality and Skills to Be a Good Patient Advocate?

From there, it will depend on the advocacy position you are looking for, and will vary depending on the type of business you work for. For example, if you want to be an

12 Most of this information pulled from www.Salary.com in August 2022 and intended for illustrative purposes only. Two salaries were determined from interviews.

advocate who helps people with their medical bills, you'll need to understand medical billing, reimbursement models, and negotiation. If you want to be a cancer navigator, you'll need to be a nurse and understand issues in oncology, neither of which you'll need for that medical billing position.

The shortest route to the answer is to find descriptions of jobs you think you would like, determine what experience and skills they are looking for, then begin working to fulfill those requirements. If you need experience you don't have, then set your sights on the positions that can feed that need. If you need education you don't have, then look into taking courses or getting a degree to fulfill that need.

If you aren't sure what is needed for a specific position, then connect with a Human Resources professional who works in the type of organization you'd like to work in (e.g. a hospital or insurance company) – and just ask.

How Can You Find Those Advocacy Jobs?

Here is some advice to help you begin a search for advocacy positions:

1. **Where to Search**
   There are a number of websites that advertise job openings. Some feature ads for every kind of job imaginable. Others are focused strictly on healthcare-related jobs.

   Here are a few places to get started:

   - www.indeed.com
   - www.ziprecruiter.com
   - www.monster.com
   - www.theladders.com
   - www.workopolis.com
   - www.careerbuilder.com
   - www.linkedin.com
   - www.snagajob.com
   - www.careervitals.com
   - www.simplyhired.com
   - www.glassdoor.com

You can also search at the online listings for your local newspaper's classifieds, your alma mater's job support site, or at local job search websites that exist in larger cities.

2. Using the Right Search Terms

The key to uncovering the available jobs is using the right search terms, depending on your requirements or wishes. Here is some good search advice:

Before you begin, write down some key words that will be useful for your ideal advocacy job. Your list might include words from the titles in Chapter Two: A Patient Advocacy Career at a Glance. It might also include the cities or counties you would like to be located in (where you now live, or a place you plan to move to.) If you don't have any geographic restrictions, then don't use them in your search terms.

Choose your terms as broadly as possible to capture as many possibilities as exist. Just because you call the position you are looking for "patient advocate" doesn't mean the organization that would be a perfect fit calls it that, too. Try variations, including those titles mentioned in Chapter Two.

3. Gaming the Search System

If you are having trouble finding the terms you're searching for, try to use just pieces of words. For example, using the term 'advocate' might mean you don't find a title that includes the word "advocacy." So, use just the portion that would be found in all the versions of the word, such as "advoca", to capture all the possibilities.

4. Limiting Your Searches

Some of the job boards and listings allow you to restrict your search to specific types of companies. For example, if you think you would like to work for a hospital, you might be able to limit your search to hospitals only.

Can't Find What You're Looking For?

If you are having trouble finding the job you want, or would qualify for, there may be several reasons:

1. If your geography, education or experience are limited, the job may just not be available.

2. Job listings come and go. Plan to search for new listings once a week or so.

3. Not all job listings are made public. Try connecting with specific employers in your area – your local hospital or a non-profit, or whatever other employer you would like to work for. See if they have job listings on their individual websites, or call their Human Resources Department to ask.

4. The truth is, most jobs are filled because of word of mouth. Try connecting with people who do the work you wish you were doing and ask them to let you know if they hear of openings. They often hear about them, or know someone has just left a position, long before any of those jobs go public (if they ever do.)

5. Don't be afraid to take a temporary job in an advocate's capacity. You might check with those same Human Resources Departments to see if they ever have openings due to a pregnancy or medical leave. Or, check with your local temp agency to see if they are ever asked to fill these kinds of positions. Even if it doesn't last more than a few months, it's a great way to gain experience, get your foot in the door, and even to determine if this career truly is what you want to choose.

Final Words and Miscellany About Getting a Job as a Patient Advocate

- **Notes on the term "navigator"**

Patient Navigator is such a great description for the work advocates do! To me, working in the private advocacy industry, it evokes the expert at the helm of the patient's ship, guiding them through the treacherous healthcare waters to safety.

But it turns out that lots of other types of healthcare guidance like the word so much, they are coopting it for their own use, making it difficult for advocates to use it.

"Patient navigator" is the term being used by the Affordable Care Act to name the people who help those who need health insurance find the right insurance. Most of these navigators are volunteers, and are called upon just once a year during open enrollment to help with that task.

"Patient navigator" is also the term being used in hospitals and cancer centers to name the nurses who hold the hands of their patients who must undergo cancer treatment. Cancer navigators are employees of the hospital, so their allegiance is to the hospital, of course. Many navigators do a wonderful job for their assigned patients, and truthfully, those patients are often well-served.

I raise this here because if you are searching for a job, and you want to use the term "navigator," beware of the pot luck nature of the results – and do your due diligence to make sure it's something you are qualified for, or interested in.

- **Building your best resumé**

I haven't attempted to provide advice on how to create a good resumé for finding your perfect advocacy job. Frankly, I'm not your best resource for that information because I've been self-employed for more than 20 years – since back in the dark ages when people were still developing resumés on real paper.

Instead, I'll provide a few resources for resumé development to help you:

- The 6 Most Important Parts of a Resume (with Examples)
  https://www.indeed.com/career-advice/resumes-cover-letters/parts-of-a-resume

- How to Boost the Odds You'll Get a New Job
  https://www.nextavenue.org/boost-odds-new-job/

- How to Build a Resume in 7 Easy Steps
  https://www.thebalancecareers.com/easy-steps-to-build-a-resume-4122296

• Notes on working for a private advocacy company

More and more patients are catching on to the fact that when it comes to allegiance, not all patient advocates can put the patient's best interest front and center. Once they understand the Allegiance Factor, they go in search of private advocates who work directly for patients.

Private, independent advocacy is a relatively new profession. Many people who make great advocates don't want to be running their own companies, but they do want to work directly for patients. This leaves them with few options for removing the employer barrier.

Recognizing that the talent pool for good advocacy exists, and recognizing that the patients who need them exist, some advocacy entrepreneurs have started advocacy companies whose core business is supplying advocates to patients. They handle all the business needs (see the outline in Chapter Six: Patient Advocates in Private Practice) and let advocates be advocates.

So, in effect, even though those advocates work for an employer, and their allegiance is to that employer – these advocates work directly for patients.

As of 2022, there are only a handful of these companies, but more are going into business every day.

If you have interest in working for one of these companies, and you can identify one that fits you – your geography, your experience, and your education, then here are some questions to ask when you score an interview:

- Do you have a parent company? (Many of these larger groups are actually the advocacy spin-off for a health insurance company, shifting the allegiance concept. Be sure that's where you want to be.)

- Are you hiring employees (meaning, paycheck, benefits, and an IRS Form W-2 at the end of the year)? Or are you hiring independent contractors (meaning, paid by the project or for hours worked, but working independently and receiving an IRS Form1099 at the end of the year)? (If they hire only independent contractors, then you will need to be self-employed. See Chapter Six: Patient Advocates in Private Practice.)

- Do you require any specific credentials? (They may limit their hiring to nurses or to certified advocates.)

- Do I need liability insurance for the work you need me to do? (If the company is a true employer, they will cover the cost of liability insurance.)

- Can you tell me what the position pays and how I can increase my rate or salary?

Then, if you're offered a job with one of these organizations, trust your gut. And if you think it's what you're looking for—give it a go!

There are links to additional information throughout this book.
To make them easier to access, I've put them all together, online,
so you can just click on them rather than typing them out.

Find access information on page 46 of this book.

Chapter Six
Patient Advocates in Private Practice

I n Chapter Five, we asked, "Who are the employers?" – meaning those people who provide patient advocacy jobs.

Now, you probably think that the answer to the question of "who is the employer?" in this chapter will be that "you are your own employer." But that is only part of the answer.

Your REAL employer, when you are self-employed as a patient advocate, is each individual who hires and pays you to do your work; usually those patients and caregivers who will hire you—employ you"— to advocate one-on-one with them, with no intermediary.

They will write you a check or give you their credit card number directly. That will be your paycheck. No reimbursements from insurance, no one else to pay you. When you are a private advocate, the individual who hires you will be your employer. (And of course, your allegiance will reflect this, too.)

This employment profile means you won't go to someone else's workplace every day – you will go to your own, whether that means a home office, or a business office in another location, and it will have the name you choose on it.

You may choose to do this as a one-person advocacy service. Or you may partner with someone else, or even be in charge of a small army of advocates – you become THEIR employer.

You may even be self-employed even though you really work for an advocacy company (see Miscellany in Chapter Five: Getting a Job as a Patient Advocate.) In this case, you may be working as an independent contractor, or subcontractor, doing work directly for patients even though that work is assigned by someone else.

No matter how you format your business, it will be your company, and you will be responsible for its success. You'll be independent, offering private services just like a private school is independent of the district in which it's found, or a lawyer in private practice is independent of a specific corporation it serves. There won't be a paycheck every other Friday, no one will withhold your taxes, and when you need a cup of coffee, it will come from your own coffee pot.

For many advocates, this spells freedom from the constraints of a boss – and from allegiance to some other entity.

To those who aren't prepared, it ends up spelling way too much stress, and eventual financial loss, or even ruin.

The key word there is "prepared."

You'll begin with a business plan which is comprised of:

- Financial projections, budgeting, money management, tax filing, and cash flow

- Insurance planning – professional liability, business liability, errors & omissions – or all three

- Plans for your contracts – legal needs, and how you will address HIPAA planning

- A marketing plan; an understanding and steps toward implementation of marketing strategy and tactics to procure the clients who will pay you

- And more.

(Find a list of resources to help you put together your business plan later in this chapter.)

How Much Money Can You Make as an Independent, Private Patient Advocate?

Those who are considering private practice would do well to consider the reality of producing income, yet so many ask the question, "What can I charge?" and think that will help them understand the income they can produce.

We're going to approach this backwards.

A private advocate, in business as one person, after two to three years of business, should be able to generate $150,000 or more per year in revenue. The highest number I've heard is just over $500,000 for one person.

But revenue is not the same as personal income. Your own income will be the result of revenue – minus all expenses. When you are in business yourself, the expenses, which include things like your phone, your travel, your liability insurance, legal expenses, marketing, even your rent, are all yours. That $150,000 might end up being $130,000 or $100,000 or $75,000 – all depending on the total expenses subtracted from the revenue. Then, of course, you'll be taxed on that income, so just like your paycheck from an employer, your real income will be a fraction of the money you actually earned.

What does it take to generate that kind of income? It takes a 40+ hour week of which 30 are billable hours, charging $100 or more per hour, for 50 weeks a year. That sounds do-able, right? And it is – but not initially. It will take you a few years to ramp up to that 'ease' of income because most of the general public doesn't even understand, yet, that private advocates, who they must pay from their own pockets, are available to help them.

Further, don't let that $100 per hour confuse you. Many advocates are charging much less than that (a real shame—they should be charging more.) Like most advocates who are just getting started, they still find it difficult to find enough clients to keep them in business.

What Skills and Education Do You Need to be a Private Advocate?

I wish I had a nickel for every potential advocate who thinks he or she, perhaps having had a background in nursing or some other clinical area, can simply hang out a sign and declare him or herself to be in the business of advocacy! Instead, most think that because they have functioned with advocacy in their heart in some other area of healthcare, they will also be successful in independent practice.

It doesn't work that way!

In Chapter Three: Do You Have the Personality and Skills to Be a Good Patient Advocate?, I listed the skills you need to do advocacy work. But they were about advocacy, not about business. To be successful in private practice you need business skills, too. Especially in the first few years, understanding how to run a business may even be more important than knowing the advocacy skills themselves.

Here is a list of the additional knowledge and skills you'll need to succeed in your independent, private advocacy practice.

- Business planning experience including (these are a repeat from the business plan section) financial projections, budgeting, money management, tax filing, capitalization, and cash flow
- Basic bookkeeping skills (especially tracking expenses and tax deductions)
- Technology management (using a computer and a smartphone, managing email, creating spreadsheets, word processing, webcasts, teleconferences, others)
- Record keeping including time tracking
- Time management
- Understanding insurance – both liability insurance for your business and how to work with your client's health or disability insurance
- Understanding the use of, and need for, business contracts, their clauses and provisions (legal)
- Marketing—an understanding and steps toward implementation of marketing strategy and tactics to procure the clients who will pay you

If these skills aren't your skills, then make sure you look for ways to fill that gap. Here are some resources for learning what you need to. Many of these programs can help you build your business plan, too, and some services are free:

- Go online to the Small Business Administration (SBA) at www.sba.gov
- Find a mentor at your local branch of SCORE: Service Corps of Retired Executives www.score.org
- Many states offer Small Business Development Centers, often housed at community colleges. Find a list at: www.sba.gov/tools/local-assistance/sbdc
- Take advocacy business workshops: www.HealthAdvocateResources.com
- Find business books for advocates available at: www.DiagKNOWsisMedia.com including *The Health Advocate's Start and Grow Your Own Practice Handbook*

Final Words and Miscellany About Private, Independent Advocacy

If you haven't been dissuaded from private advocacy yet – great! I'm so happy about that! (Told you – I'm biased.)

So here are a few points to consider if private, independent advocacy is still under your consideration:

• **What About the Rules?**

One key to success in private advocacy: you can't be afraid to break the rules and make up your own when necessary.

I say this because I've found over the years that many people who want to become advocates just can't make the leap. The problem isn't about business, and it isn't about caring or passion or any of those important attributes. Instead it's because they've been conditioned to respond to certain problems in a certain way. But that may not work for your client.

This most frequently happens to those who have worked in a bureaucracy where the rules were the rules. It's especially difficult for nurses who have had orders barked at them for long careers; then they want to shift to private advocacy after they've reached a certain age – and many just can't make that leap. They are waiting for someone to tell them what to do. Or they think that patients will just come to them (which they did when these folks were hospital or doctor practice nurses.) In private advocacy it just doesn't work that way.

I call it "hustle." Advocates need to find alternate routes, ask alternate questions, and realize that independent advocacy instead requires creative thinking – coloring outside the lines, thinking outside that proverbial box.

If you think you'd like to be a private, independent advocate, make sure you can operate outside the rules, with the objectivity you'll need to see the world from the patient-client's point of view.

• **With Private Advocacy, Patients Take on a New Name**

That is, once they become private pay, and especially because advocates are not medical, and do not offer medical services, your patients will instead become your "clients" (or even "customers".) The distinction is important for a number of reasons which I won't describe here. But you'll find your new world of advocacy will shift that thinking for you – from patients to clients – it's a mindset, and important for legal and insurance reasons.

If all this business stuff sounds foreign or daunting, please take time to check out the resources at the end of this book. They'll go a long way toward taking the "sting" out of these challenges.

Chapter Seven

Step by Step to Making Your Choice

So now that you've waded through so many questions and possibilities, I can imagine that your head may be spinning. You thought it would all be so much clearer, right? But maybe not.

I want to help you clarify your own thoughts through a series of questions, step by step, to making your decision about how to proceed. There are no right or wrong answers to the questions you're about to answer, except that they are right or wrong for you.

Feel free to circle or write the answers right here in your book. If you'd like to print off a copy of these questions, you can do so from here:

https://DiagKNOWsisMedia.com/downloads/choose.pdf

1. Determining whether or not you'll make a good patient advocate:

In Chapter Three you'll find a list of personality and personal attributes that advocates must have to be successful. Let's see how you stack up against those attributes:

a. I am a people person.		Yes	No
b. I am a good listener.		Yes	No
c. I am empathetic.		Yes	No
d. I am ethical and trustworthy.		Yes	No
e. I have patience and compassion.		Yes	No

f. I am a creative problem solver and decision maker.Yes   No

g. I am a confident communicator.   Yes   No

h. I have a thick skin.   Yes   No

Scoring:

If you circled NO for any of the attributes, then assess that missing attribute against its explanation in Chapter Three. See if there is a way you can proceed to fill that gap. Some attributes will be easier than others to overcome (it's easier to develop a thick skin than it is to become empathetic.)

If you can determine with confidence that you have or can develop all these attributes – then move on to the next question about pursuing advocacy as a career. If not, then patient advocacy is probably not for you.

2. Determining your advocacy skill and knowledge level

Also in Chapter Three you'll find a list of skills and knowledge you will need to be an effective advocate. Unlike the personality traits, these can be learned through study. The key is to figure out what you do know – vs – what you don't know – and then to make a plan to fill that gap.

Circle the skills you DO NOT have – as a way of identifying what gaps to fill.

a. Knowledge of how the healthcare system works

b. Knowledge of how patients and caregivers think, and the ability to put oneself in their shoes (empathy and point of view)

c. Knowledge of how doctors' offices, hospitals, other facilities and healthcare organizations function

d. Knowledge of how health insurance works, both for and against patients

e. Health system navigation knowledge

f. Knowledge of HIPAA basics

g. Shared decision making and expectation management skills

h. Medical billing, insurance claims and reimbursement systems knowledge

i. Creative problem solving

j.   Research skills and good resources– for learning about diagnoses or treatment options, finding good professionals to work with and more

k.   Professionalism

l.   A solid commitment to, and understanding of customer service tenets

m. Good telephone manners

n.   Be well-spoken

o.   Strong handshake (an air of confidence)

p.   Facilitation / Negotiation / bargaining/mediation skills for working with patients and their loved ones, or encouraging medical personal to see things your way

Which ones did you circle? If you circled some of these, like being professional, having a strong handshake, or being well-spoken, then this is just a step toward upgrading your behavior in business settings. Ask someone you admire to tutor you in these finer aspects of business success.

Other skills and knowledge points can be learned from taking classes or workshops, reading books, or just reading everything you can get your hands on, online. For example, understanding the basics of HIPAA (privacy policy) or how the reimbursement system works (the ways doctors and facilities get paid) – both are information that is found in many places.

If you circled more than two of three of these skills, then you'll want to cover those gaps before you apply for an advocacy job or hang out your own shingle as a private advocate. You can't succeed without this knowledge.

3. Your Ethics and Allegiance

In Chapter Four, we took at a look at the Allegiance Factor, conflicts of interest, and how that interfaces with advocacy and patients.

a.   Do you understand the Allegiance Factor?

b.   Do you understand, agree, and abide by advocate's Codes of Ethics?

c.   Are you invested in helping these tenets govern your work with patients? If you answer no to this question, then please – don't enter advocacy as a career. You would be doing other advocates no favor. We don't ever want to become the used car salespeople of healthcare.

4. Your Current Work Situation

If you've made it through the questions to this point and are still enthused about advocacy – that's great! Now it's time to determine what direction you'll take your career based on the reality of your life right now.

If you know already that you want to work for an employer (don't care to, or aren't able to start your own business) then you have reached the end of your questions. You know what direction to take, so return to Chapter Five and get started!

If you think you'd like to go into private advocacy, here are some questions that can help you determine if it's a possibility for you:

a.   Do you need a regular paycheck? Or can you live on irregular payments, when clients are ready to pay you? If you can live with irregular payments, then go on to "b."

b.   Do you have enough money in the bank to carry you for six months (or longer) without any income? While some advocates find paying clients right away, others must do plenty of marketing to uncover people who are willing to pay them.

   Note! "Pay them" is the key. There are lots of people who need help, and lots of people who would like you to help them. But too many advocates base their choice to go into business on how many people want or need help – vs – how many are willing to pay for help. There is a huge difference.

   Further, the start-up costs to a business can take a real bite out of your bank accounts. Part of the reality check here is that no banks or regular lenders are willing to lend money for a business, or business owner, who is untested. If you want to borrow money, you'll need to do so from yourself or your rich uncle.

   If you've determined that yes, you can carry yourself and your expenses for a while, then let's move on to our next question.

c.   Let's look at your business skills. Like in Question 2, circle the skills you don't feel competent in – this will identify the holes you need to fill:

   •   Business planning experience including (these are a repeat from the business plan section) financial projections, budgeting, money management, tax filing, capitalization, and cash flow

   •   Basic bookkeeping skills (especially understanding tax deductions, tracking expenses)

   •   Technology management (using a computer, using a smartphone, managing email, creating spreadsheets, word processing, webcasts, teleconferences, others)

- Record keeping, time tracking

- Time management

- Understanding insurance – both liability insurance for your business and how to work with your client's health or disability insurance

- Understanding the use of, and need for, business contracts, their clauses and provisions (legal)

- Marketing; an understanding and steps toward implementation of marketing strategy and tactics to procure the clients who will pay you

Chapter Four also contained a list of places you can get help with each of these aspects of business.

If you circled more than two of these competencies, you will want to hang on to your day job for a while until you have developed them.

d. Here is your last question to help you decide whether you can succeed in private, independent advocacy: Can you ask for money, send an invoice, and expect to be paid for doing your advocacy work?

This one question stymies so many people. They are great advocates. They are able to accomplish a great deal while helping others. In many cases, they tell me they've been advocating for friends and loved ones for decades. They KNOW they can succeed in private advocacy! .... But then.... When it comes time to ask for a signature on a contract with a client, and that involves outlining costs and asking for money.... Well.... They just can't make that leap.

Can you? Because if you go into private advocacy, you will have to do so. If you can't picture yourself asking for money, and if you can't actually do it – and follow through – and pursue money owed to you – then you will not succeed in private practice.

That's the final question to help you make your choice. By now you should know just what direction to take for yourself, and whether or not it's time to take the plunge.

There are links to additional information throughout this book. To make them easier to access, I've put them all together, online, so you can just click on them rather than typing them out.

Find access information on page 46 of this book.

Chapter Eight

Some Final Advice about Choosing a Career in Patient Advocacy

f you know you'd like to be a an advocate, but you either aren't in a position to give up your regular paycheck, or you can't find the job that's right for you right away, then here are a couple of ways to make the transition more gradually:

- Begin taking some of your gap courses while still employed in your old job.

- Do some volunteer advocacy. It's easy to get this started if you aren't doing so already. You can mention your willingness to friends, or at church, or at your next book club meeting, or anywhere else that makes sense to you.

  The one important point you must make to each person you help as a volunteer is that your volunteerism is short-term. Your plans are to begin charging for your services by ____ (add your own date). That way it will be easier to make that transition from free services to paid services when the time comes.

- Talk to others who are working as advocates and see what advice they can give you to get you started. What did they do right that they recommend you do, too? What do they wish they had known that will help prepare you or save you grief?

- Even if you plan to become a private advocate, it can be great experience to work in a hospital or for an insurance company first. This kind of on-the-job training will fill in some of your knowledge gaps, and will also help you learn what does work and (probably more importantly) what doesn't work well for the patients you work with. Further, your understanding of the Allegiance Factor will come into even sharper focus.

That's it! I wish you the best of luck in your new advocacy pursuit. As mentioned before, I love advocates! I want you to succeed whether you do so through an employer, or in your own private practice. Patients need you.

If you will, send me a quick note about YOUR choice! I'd love to hear from you. (trisha@epadvocate.org)

Resources

Additional Information for You

You'll find resources throughout this book, including many links to additional information.

I've made all those links available from one place to make your search for additional information easier. Whether you're reading the softcover or e-book version of this book, you might find this helpful.

Choosing a Career in Health or Patient Advocacy Resources

> **diagknowsismedia.com/access/access-bpa-resources/**

You'll find the links found throughout this book, plus the additional resources below. The benefit to accessing them online is the ease of linking; otherwise the information is identical.

Additional Resources:

Articles:

- Tips on How to Become a Patient Advocate
  https://www.geteducated.com/career-center/detail/patient-advocate

- Working In Retirement: How To Be A Patient Advocate
  https://www.nextavenue.org/working-retirement-how-be-patient-advocate/

- An Overview of Patient Advocacy
  https://aphadvocates.org/profession-overview/

- How to Become a Patient Advocate or Navigator
  www.verywellhealth.com/how-to-become-a-patient-advocate-or-navigator-2614922

- Find additional articles from media about the profession of advocacy and individuals who are making progress: https://www.aphadvocates.org/members-in-the-news/

- Find more general articles about patient advocacy, becoming a patient advocate, and starting a patient or health advocacy business. https://aphablog.com/getting-started/

Books

Links to all these books can be found at: **www.diagKNOWsisMedia.com** or can be purchased through Amazon, B&N and other bookstores, online or off.

- You Bet Your Life! The 10 Mistakes Every Patient Makes
(How to Fix Them to Get the Healthcare You Deserve)
- You Bet Your Life! The Top 10 Reasons You Need a Professional Patient Advocate by Your Side

This *Choosing a Career* book is #1 in the Health Advocacy Career Series.

Also available:

2. The Health Advocate's Start and Grow Your Own Practice Handbook **(see offer below*)**

3. The Health Advocate's Basic Marketing Handbook

4. The Health Advocate's Advanced Marketing Handbook

*Coupon!

Purchase the second book in this series:

The Health Advocate's Start and Grow Own Practice Handbook

Get $5 off (includes free shipping!)

diagknowsismedia.com/product/sgop/

Use coupon code:

bpa-purchase-5off-sgop

About the Author

When Trisha Torrey was diagnosed with a rare, aggressive lymphoma in 2004, she was a marketing consultant who knew almost nothing about healthcare. She was naïve to the dysfunction of the American healthcare system that was tasked with treating her.

But she got smart, fast. She learned that the possibility of excellent care was too easily and frequently eclipsed by miscommunication and mistakes. She also learned that if she didn't stick up for herself, and insist on the help she needed, she would not get it. The more empowered she became, the more she realized there was a possibility she had no lymphoma. Eventually she proved she was right; she had no cancer. They had been wrong—a misdiagnosis. To this day, she has never had any form of treatment.

Once Trisha put that "no cancer" odyssey behind her, she decided it was up to her to apply her skills to teaching others how to navigate the dangerous landscape of American healthcare. She sold her marketing company in 2006 to devote herself full time to the cause.

Today Trisha calls herself "Every Patient's Advocate." She is the founder and former director of AdvoConnection.com and the Alliance of Professional Health Advocates which support the business aspects of a health advocate's work. She speaks to groups of patients and professionals, and teaches workshops. She is the author of six books, all relating to advocacy, whether it is self-advocacy or becoming a patient advocate.

Trisha has been quoted by CNN, NBC, Fox, MSNBC, the Wall Street Journal, Health Magazine, O Magazine, U.S. News and World Report, NPR, Scientific American, Angie's List Magazine, Bottom Line Publications, and others. She is a contributing author to *Our Bodies Ourselves* (40-year anniversary edition.)

She lives in Florida with her husband, Butch, and her rescue mini-mutt, Banjo. When she's not doing her patient advocacy thing, she enjoys playing golf, travel, gardening, and working in stained glass.

Twitter:	@TrishaTorrey
Facebook:	https://www.facebook.com/Trisha.Torrey
LinkedIn:	www.LinkedIn.com/TrishaTorrey
Web:	TrishaTorrey.com

Made in the USA
Middletown, DE
14 January 2023

22170143R00029